Doctor

Jeff Barger

Rourke
Education
rourkee

BEFORE AND DURING READING ACTIVITIES

Before Reading: *Building Background Knowledge and Vocabulary*

Building background knowledge can help children process new information and build upon what they already know. Before reading a book, it is important to tap into what children already know about the topic. This will help them develop their vocabulary and increase their reading comprehension.

Questions and Activities to Build Background Knowledge:

1. Look at the front cover of the book and read the title. What do you think this book will be about?
2. What do you already know about this topic?
3. Take a book walk and skim the pages. Look at the table of contents, photographs, captions, and bold words. Did these text features give you any information or predictions about what you will read in this book?

Vocabulary: *Vocabulary Is Key to Reading Comprehension*

Use the following directions to prompt a conversation about each word.
- Read the vocabulary words.
- What comes to mind when you see each word?
- What do you think each word means?

Vocabulary Words:
- *examines*
- *patient*
- *temperature*
- *x-rays*

During Reading: *Reading for Meaning and Understanding*

To achieve deep comprehension of a book, children are encouraged to use close reading strategies. During reading, it is important to have children stop and make connections. These connections result in deeper analysis and understanding of a book.

 Close Reading a Text

During reading, have children stop and talk about the following:
- Any confusing parts
- unknown words
- text, text to self, text to world connections
- idea in each chapter or heading

n to use context clues to determine the meaning of any unknown words. These children learn to analyze the text more thoroughly as they read.

reading this book, turn to the next-to-last page for an After Reading Activity.

Table of Contents

Community Helpers 4

A Visit to the Doctor. 8

How Doctors Help. 12

Activity 21

Photo Glossary 22

Index 23

After Reading Activity. 23

About the Author 24

Community Helpers

Community helpers are all around us. They make our lives better.

People who live or work in the same area are part of a community.

Doctors help when you are sick.

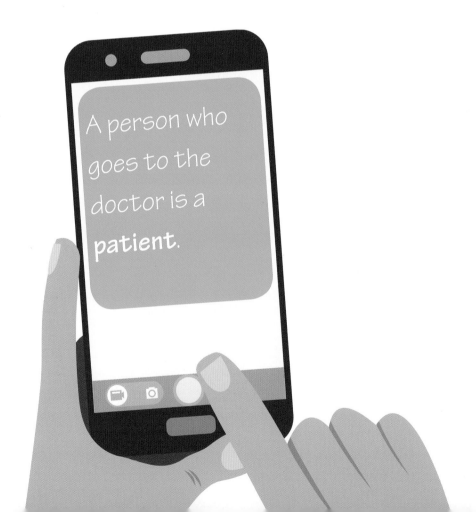

A person who goes to the doctor is a **patient**.

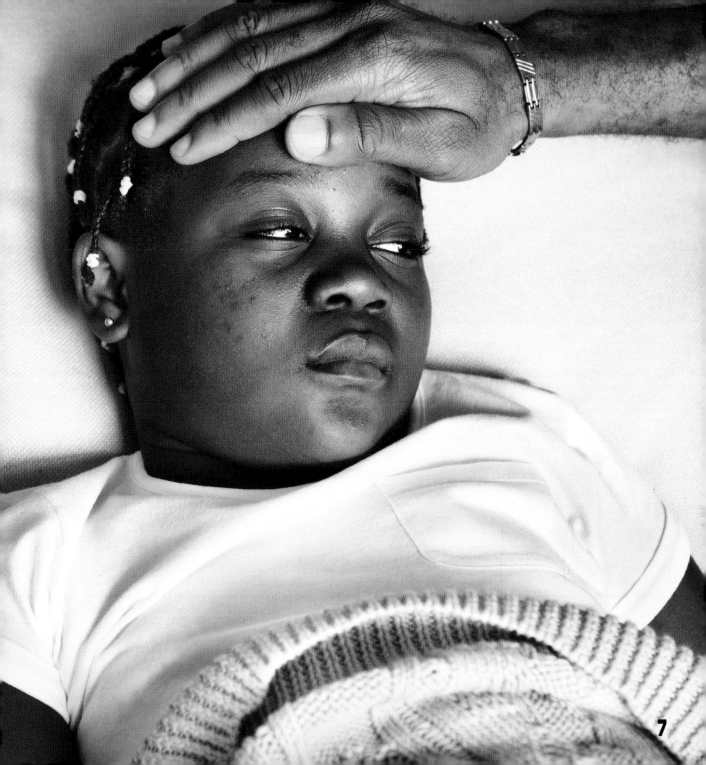

A Visit to the Doctor

You have a sore throat.

You go to the doctor.

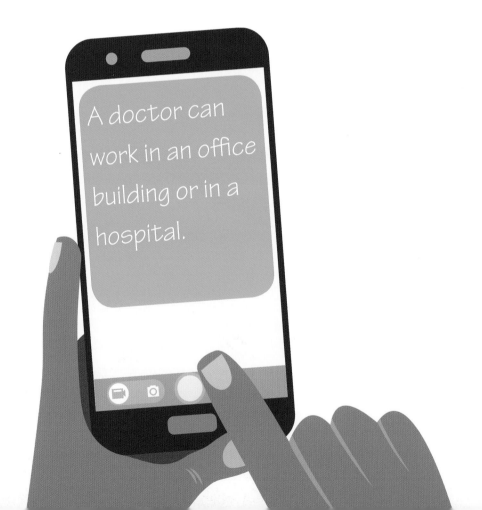

A doctor can work in an office building or in a hospital.

A nurse checks your **temperature**. They use a tool. It goes under your tongue.

The tool is called a thermometer.

How Doctors Help

You hear a knock on the door. The doctor comes in. They ask, "What hurts?"

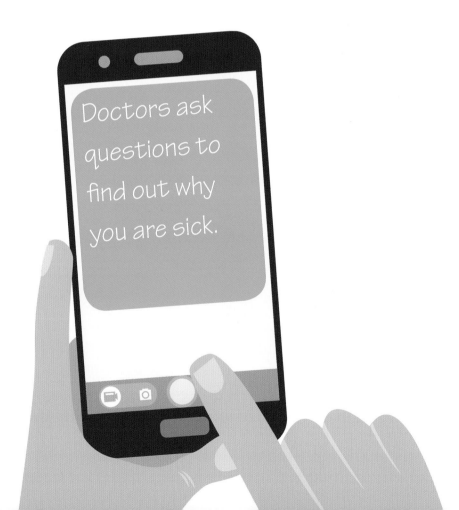

Doctors ask questions to find out why you are sick.

The doctor **examines** you.

They check your ears.

A doctor checks different parts of your body during an exam.

You open your mouth.

The doctor checks your throat.

The doctor writes a note.

It is called a *prescription*.

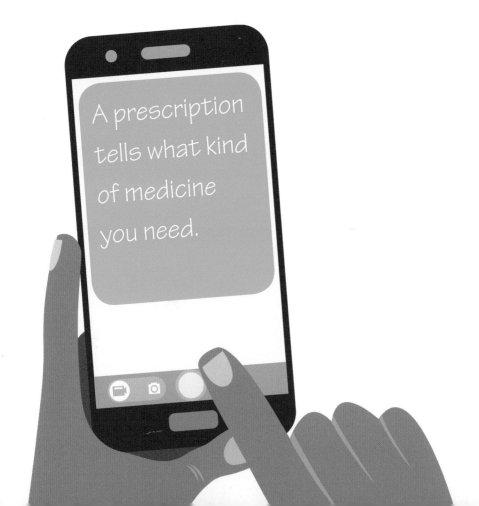

A prescription tells what kind of medicine you need.

R X MEDICAL CENTER

Doctors also take **x-rays**. They perform surgery.

Doctors help us stay healthy.

Activity

Interview with a Doctor

An interview is when you ask someone questions. Make a plan to interview your doctor!

Supplies
- paper folded in two
- markers or crayons
- pencil

Directions

1. Use the paper and markers or crayons to make a card for your doctor. On the front, write: Thank you for taking care of me!

2. Think of questions to ask your doctor. For example, "How did you become a doctor?" could be a question.

3. Write three questions inside the card you made.

4. Deliver the card when you visit your doctor. Ask your doctor to answer each question on the card.

Photo Glossary

examines (ig-ZAM-ins): Checks a person's body to see if it is healthy and normal.

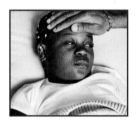

patient (PAY-shuhnt): A person who is getting treatment from a doctor or other health provider.

temperature (TEM-pur-uh-chur): The degree of heat inside a person's body.

x-rays (EKS-rays): Pictures of the inside of a person's body.

Index

community   4

exam   14

hospital   8

office   8

prescription   18

surgery   20

After Reading Activity

Pretend you are a doctor. Make a poster for your office that shows three important ways to stay healthy.

About the Author

Jeff Barger is an author, blogger, and literacy specialist. He lives in North Carolina. He likes a good bowl of chicken soup when he is sick. And a television remote control.

www.rourkeeducationalmedia.com

Edited by: Kim Thompson
Cover and interior design by: Kathy Walsh

Photo Credits: Cover, title page, p.11, 20, 22: ©Steve Debenport; p.5, 7: ©Rawpixel.com; p.9: SeventyFour; p.13: ©DragonImages; p.15, 22: ©Catherine Yeulet; p.17: ©RicardoImagen; p.19: ©stevecoleimages; p. 20, 22: ©Henk Badenhorst

Library of Congress PCN Data

Doctor / Jeff Barger
(Community Helpers)
ISBN 978-1-73161-421-6 (hard cover)(alk. paper)
ISBN 978-1-73161-216-8 (soft cover)
ISBN 978-1-73161-526-8 (e-Book)
ISBN 978-1-73161-631-9 (ePub)
Library of Congress Control Number: 2019932038

Rourke Educational Media
Printed in the United States of America,
North Mankato, Minnesota